Horizontal Merger Guidelines

U.S. Department of Justice

and the

Federal Trade Commission

Issued: August 19, 2010

Table of Contents

1. Overview 1

2. Evidence of Adverse Competitive Effects 2
2.1 Types of Evidence 3
2.1.1 Actual Effects Observed in Consummated Mergers 3
2.1.2 Direct Comparisons Based on Experience 3
2.1.3 Market Shares and Concentration in a Relevant Market 3
2.1.4 Substantial Head-to-Head Competition 3
2.1.5 Disruptive Role of a Merging Party 3
2.2 Sources of Evidence 4
2.2.1 Merging Parties 4
2.2.2 Customers 5
2.2.3 Other Industry Participants and Observers 5

3. Targeted Customers and Price Discrimination 6

4. Market Definition 7
4.1 Product Market Definition 8
4.1.1 The Hypothetical Monopolist Test 8
4.1.2 Benchmark Prices and SSNIP Size 10
4.1.3 Implementing the Hypothetical Monopolist Test 11
4.1.4 Product Market Definition with Targeted Customers 12
4.2 Geographic Market Definition 13
4.2.1 Geographic Markets Based on the Locations of Suppliers 13
4.2.2 Geographic Markets Based on the Locations of Customers 14

5. Market Participants, Market Shares, and Market Concentration 15
5.1 Market Participants 15
5.2 Market Shares 16
5.3 Market Concentration 18

6. Unilateral Effects 20
6.1 Pricing of Differentiated Products 20
6.2 Bargaining and Auctions 22
6.3 Capacity and Output for Homogeneous Products 22
6.4 Innovation and Product Variety 23

7. Coordinated Effects 24
7.1 Impact of Merger on Coordinated Interaction 25
7.2 Evidence a Market is Vulnerable to Coordinated Conduct 25

8. Powerful Buyers 27

9.	Entry	27
9.1	Timeliness	29
9.2	Likelihood	29
9.3	Sufficiency	29
10.	Efficiencies	29
11.	Failure and Exiting Assets	32
12.	Mergers of Competing Buyers	32
13.	Partial Acquisitions	33

1. Overview

These Guidelines outline the principal analytical techniques, practices, and the enforcement policy of the Department of Justice and the Federal Trade Commission (the "Agencies") with respect to mergers and acquisitions involving actual or potential competitors ("horizontal mergers") under the federal antitrust laws.[1] The relevant statutory provisions include Section 7 of the Clayton Act, 15 U.S.C. § 18, Sections 1 and 2 of the Sherman Act, 15 U.S.C. §§ 1, 2, and Section 5 of the Federal Trade Commission Act, 15 U.S.C. § 45. Most particularly, Section 7 of the Clayton Act prohibits mergers if "in any line of commerce or in any activity affecting commerce in any section of the country, the effect of such acquisition may be substantially to lessen competition, or to tend to create a monopoly."

The Agencies seek to identify and challenge competitively harmful mergers while avoiding unnecessary interference with mergers that are either competitively beneficial or neutral. Most merger analysis is necessarily predictive, requiring an assessment of what will likely happen if a merger proceeds as compared to what will likely happen if it does not. Given this inherent need for prediction, these Guidelines reflect the congressional intent that merger enforcement should interdict competitive problems in their incipiency and that certainty about anticompetitive effect is seldom possible and not required for a merger to be illegal.

These Guidelines describe the principal analytical techniques and the main types of evidence on which the Agencies usually rely to predict whether a horizontal merger may substantially lessen competition. They are not intended to describe how the Agencies analyze cases other than horizontal mergers. These Guidelines are intended to assist the business community and antitrust practitioners by increasing the transparency of the analytical process underlying the Agencies' enforcement decisions. They may also assist the courts in developing an appropriate framework for interpreting and applying the antitrust laws in the horizontal merger context.

These Guidelines should be read with the awareness that merger analysis does not consist of uniform application of a single methodology. Rather, it is a fact-specific process through which the Agencies, guided by their extensive experience, apply a range of analytical tools to the reasonably available and reliable evidence to evaluate competitive concerns in a limited period of time. Where these Guidelines provide examples, they are illustrative and do not exhaust the applications of the relevant principle.[2]

---

[1] These Guidelines replace the Horizontal Merger Guidelines issued in 1992, revised in 1997. They reflect the ongoing accumulation of experience at the Agencies. The Commentary on the Horizontal Merger Guidelines issued by the Agencies in 2006 remains a valuable supplement to these Guidelines. These Guidelines may be revised from time to time as necessary to reflect significant changes in enforcement policy, to clarify existing policy, or to reflect new learning. These Guidelines do not cover vertical or other types of non-horizontal acquisitions.

[2] These Guidelines are not intended to describe how the Agencies will conduct the litigation of cases they decide to bring. Although relevant in that context, these Guidelines neither dictate nor exhaust the range of evidence the Agencies may introduce in litigation.

The unifying theme of these Guidelines is that mergers should not be permitted to create, enhance, or entrench market power or to facilitate its exercise. For simplicity of exposition, these Guidelines generally refer to all of these effects as enhancing market power. A merger enhances market power if it is likely to encourage one or more firms to raise price, reduce output, diminish innovation, or otherwise harm customers as a result of diminished competitive constraints or incentives. In evaluating how a merger will likely change a firm's behavior, the Agencies focus primarily on how the merger affects conduct that would be most profitable for the firm.

A merger can enhance market power simply by eliminating competition between the merging parties. This effect can arise even if the merger causes no changes in the way other firms behave. Adverse competitive effects arising in this manner are referred to as "unilateral effects." A merger also can enhance market power by increasing the risk of coordinated, accommodating, or interdependent behavior among rivals. Adverse competitive effects arising in this manner are referred to as "coordinated effects." In any given case, either or both types of effects may be present, and the distinction between them may be blurred.

These Guidelines principally describe how the Agencies analyze mergers between rival suppliers that may enhance their market power as sellers. Enhancement of market power by sellers often elevates the prices charged to customers. For simplicity of exposition, these Guidelines generally discuss the analysis in terms of such price effects. Enhanced market power can also be manifested in non-price terms and conditions that adversely affect customers, including reduced product quality, reduced product variety, reduced service, or diminished innovation. Such non-price effects may coexist with price effects, or can arise in their absence. When the Agencies investigate whether a merger may lead to a substantial lessening of non-price competition, they employ an approach analogous to that used to evaluate price competition. Enhanced market power may also make it more likely that the merged entity can profitably and effectively engage in exclusionary conduct. Regardless of how enhanced market power likely would be manifested, the Agencies normally evaluate mergers based on their impact on customers. The Agencies examine effects on either or both of the direct customers and the final consumers. The Agencies presume, absent convincing evidence to the contrary, that adverse effects on direct customers also cause adverse effects on final consumers.

Enhancement of market power by buyers, sometimes called "monopsony power," has adverse effects comparable to enhancement of market power by sellers. The Agencies employ an analogous framework to analyze mergers between rival purchasers that may enhance their market power as buyers. See Section 12.

2. Evidence of Adverse Competitive Effects

The Agencies consider any reasonably available and reliable evidence to address the central question of whether a merger may substantially lessen competition. This section discusses several categories and sources of evidence that the Agencies, in their experience, have found most informative in predicting the likely competitive effects of mergers. The list provided here is not exhaustive. In any given case, reliable evidence may be available in only some categories or from some sources. For each category of evidence, the Agencies consider evidence indicating that the merger may enhance competition as well as evidence indicating that it may lessen competition.

2.1 Types of Evidence

2.1.1   Actual Effects Observed in Consummated Mergers

When evaluating a consummated merger, the ultimate issue is not only whether adverse competitive effects have already resulted from the merger, but also whether such effects are likely to arise in the future. Evidence of observed post-merger price increases or other changes adverse to customers is given substantial weight. The Agencies evaluate whether such changes are anticompetitive effects resulting from the merger, in which case they can be dispositive. However, a consummated merger may be anticompetitive even if such effects have not yet been observed, perhaps because the merged firm may be aware of the possibility of post-merger antitrust review and moderating its conduct. Consequently, the Agencies also consider the same types of evidence they consider when evaluating unconsummated mergers.

2.1.2   Direct Comparisons Based on Experience

The Agencies look for historical events, or "natural experiments," that are informative regarding the competitive effects of the merger. For example, the Agencies may examine the impact of recent mergers, entry, expansion, or exit in the relevant market. Effects of analogous events in similar markets may also be informative.

The Agencies also look for reliable evidence based on variations among similar markets. For example, if the merging firms compete in some locales but not others, comparisons of prices charged in regions where they do and do not compete may be informative regarding post-merger prices. In some cases, however, prices are set on such a broad geographic basis that such comparisons are not informative. The Agencies also may examine how prices in similar markets vary with the number of significant competitors in those markets.

2.1.3   Market Shares and Concentration in a Relevant Market

The Agencies give weight to the merging parties' market shares in a relevant market, the level of concentration, and the change in concentration caused by the merger. See Sections 4 and 5. Mergers that cause a significant increase in concentration and result in highly concentrated markets are presumed to be likely to enhance market power, but this presumption can be rebutted by persuasive evidence showing that the merger is unlikely to enhance market power.

2.1.4   Substantial Head-to-Head Competition

The Agencies consider whether the merging firms have been, or likely will become absent the merger, substantial head-to-head competitors. Such evidence can be especially relevant for evaluating adverse unilateral effects, which result directly from the loss of that competition. See Section 6. This evidence can also inform market definition. See Section 4.

2.1.5   Disruptive Role of a Merging Party

The Agencies consider whether a merger may lessen competition by eliminating a "maverick" firm, i.e., a firm that plays a disruptive role in the market to the benefit of customers. For example, if one of the merging firms has a strong incumbency position and the other merging firm threatens to disrupt market conditions with a new technology or business model, their merger can involve the loss of actual or potential competition. Likewise, one of the merging firms may have the incentive to take the lead in price cutting or other competitive conduct or to resist increases in industry prices. A firm that may discipline prices based on its ability and incentive to expand production rapidly using available capacity also can be a maverick, as can a firm that has often resisted otherwise prevailing industry norms to cooperate on price setting or other terms of competition.

2.2 Sources of Evidence

The Agencies consider many sources of evidence in their merger analysis. The most common sources of reasonably available and reliable evidence are the merging parties, customers, other industry participants, and industry observers.

2.2.1 Merging Parties

The Agencies typically obtain substantial information from the merging parties. This information can take the form of documents, testimony, or data, and can consist of descriptions of competitively relevant conditions or reflect actual business conduct and decisions. Documents created in the normal course are more probative than documents created as advocacy materials in merger review. Documents describing industry conditions can be informative regarding the operation of the market and how a firm identifies and assesses its rivals, particularly when business decisions are made in reliance on the accuracy of those descriptions. The business decisions taken by the merging firms also can be informative about industry conditions. For example, if a firm sets price well above incremental cost, that normally indicates either that the firm believes its customers are not highly sensitive to price (not in itself of antitrust concern, see Section 4.1.3[3]) or that the firm and its rivals are engaged in coordinated interaction (see Section 7). Incremental cost depends on the relevant increment in output as well as on the time period involved, and in the case of large increments and sustained changes in output it may include some costs that would be fixed for smaller increments of output or shorter time periods.

Explicit or implicit evidence that the merging parties intend to raise prices, reduce output or capacity, reduce product quality or variety, withdraw products or delay their introduction, or curtail research and development efforts after the merger, or explicit or implicit evidence that the ability to engage in such conduct motivated the merger, can be highly informative in evaluating the likely effects of a merger. Likewise, the Agencies look for reliable evidence that the merger is likely to result in efficiencies. The Agencies give careful consideration to the views of individuals whose responsibilities, expertise, and experience relating to the issues in question provide particular indicia of reliability. The financial terms of the transaction may also be informative regarding competitive effects. For example, a purchase price in excess of the acquired firm's stand-alone market value may indicate that the acquiring firm is paying a premium because it expects to be able to reduce competition or to achieve efficiencies.

---

[3] High margins commonly arise for products that are significantly differentiated. Products involving substantial fixed costs typically will be developed only if suppliers expect there to be enough differentiation to support margins sufficient to cover those fixed costs. High margins can be consistent with incumbent firms earning competitive returns.

2.2.2   Customers

Customers can provide a variety of information to the Agencies, ranging from information about their own purchasing behavior and choices to their views about the effects of the merger itself.

Information from customers about how they would likely respond to a price increase, and the relative attractiveness of different products or suppliers, may be highly relevant, especially when corroborated by other evidence such as historical purchasing patterns and practices. Customers also can provide valuable information about the impact of historical events such as entry by a new supplier.

The conclusions of well-informed and sophisticated customers on the likely impact of the merger itself can also help the Agencies investigate competitive effects, because customers typically feel the consequences of both competitively beneficial and competitively harmful mergers. In evaluating such evidence, the Agencies are mindful that customers may oppose, or favor, a merger for reasons unrelated to the antitrust issues raised by that merger.

When some customers express concerns about the competitive effects of a merger while others view the merger as beneficial or neutral, the Agencies take account of this divergence in using the information provided by customers and consider the likely reasons for such divergence of views. For example, if for regulatory reasons some customers cannot buy imported products, while others can, a merger between domestic suppliers may harm the former customers even if it leaves the more flexible customers unharmed. See Section 3.

When direct customers of the merging firms compete against one another in a downstream market, their interests may not be aligned with the interests of final consumers, especially if the direct customers expect to pass on any anticompetitive price increase. A customer that is protected from adverse competitive effects by a long-term contract, or otherwise relatively immune from the merger's harmful effects, may even welcome an anticompetitive merger that provides that customer with a competitive advantage over its downstream rivals.

> *Example 1:* As a result of the merger, Customer C will experience a price increase for an input used in producing its final product, raising its costs. Customer C's rivals use this input more intensively than Customer C, and the same price increase applied to them will raise their costs more than it raises Customer C's costs. On balance, Customer C may benefit from the merger even though the merger involves a substantial lessening of competition.

2.2.3   Other Industry Participants and Observers

Suppliers, indirect customers, distributors, other industry participants, and industry analysts can also provide information helpful to a merger inquiry. The interests of firms selling products complementary to those offered by the merging firms often are well aligned with those of customers, making their informed views valuable.

Information from firms that are rivals to the merging parties can help illuminate how the market operates. The interests of rival firms often diverge from the interests of customers, since customers normally lose, but rival firms gain, if the merged entity raises its prices. For that reason, the Agencies do not routinely rely on the overall views of rival firms regarding the competitive effects of the merger. However, rival firms may provide relevant facts, and even their overall views may be instructive, especially in cases where the Agencies are concerned that the merged entity may engage in exclusionary conduct.

> *Example 2:* Merging Firms A and B operate in a market in which network effects are significant, implying that any firm's product is significantly more valuable if it commands a large market share or if it is interconnected with others that in aggregate command such a share. Prior to the merger, they and their rivals voluntarily interconnect with one another. The merger would create an entity with a large enough share that a strategy of ending voluntary interconnection would have a dangerous probability of creating monopoly power in this market. The interests of rivals and of consumers would be broadly aligned in preventing such a merger.

3. Targeted Customers and Price Discrimination

When examining possible adverse competitive effects from a merger, the Agencies consider whether those effects vary significantly for different customers purchasing the same or similar products. Such differential impacts are possible when sellers can discriminate, e.g., by profitably raising price to certain targeted customers but not to others. The possibility of price discrimination influences market definition (see Section 4), the measurement of market shares (see Section 5), and the evaluation of competitive effects (see Sections 6 and 7).

When price discrimination is feasible, adverse competitive effects on targeted customers can arise, even if such effects will not arise for other customers. A price increase for targeted customers may be profitable even if a price increase for all customers would not be profitable because too many other customers would substitute away. When discrimination is reasonably likely, the Agencies may evaluate competitive effects separately by type of customer. The Agencies may have access to information unavailable to customers that is relevant to evaluating whether discrimination is reasonably likely.

For price discrimination to be feasible, two conditions typically must be met: differential pricing and limited arbitrage.

First, the suppliers engaging in price discrimination must be able to price differently to targeted customers than to other customers. This may involve identification of individual customers to which different prices are offered or offering different prices to different types of customers based on observable characteristics.

> *Example 3:* Suppliers can distinguish large buyers from small buyers. Large buyers are more likely than small buyers to self-supply in response to a significant price increase. The merger may lead to price discrimination against small buyers, harming them, even if large buyers are not harmed. Such discrimination can occur even if there is no discrete gap in size between the classes of large and small buyers.

In other cases, suppliers may be unable to distinguish among different types of customers but can offer multiple products that sort customers based on their purchase decisions.

Second, the targeted customers must not be able to defeat the price increase of concern by arbitrage, e.g., by purchasing indirectly from or through other customers. Arbitrage may be difficult if it would void warranties or make service more difficult or costly for customers. Arbitrage is inherently impossible for many services. Arbitrage between customers at different geographic locations may be impractical due to transportation costs. Arbitrage on a modest scale may be possible but sufficiently costly or limited that it would not deter or defeat a discriminatory pricing strategy.

4. Market Definition

When the Agencies identify a potential competitive concern with a horizontal merger, market definition plays two roles. First, market definition helps specify the line of commerce and section of the country in which the competitive concern arises. In any merger enforcement action, the Agencies will normally identify one or more relevant markets in which the merger may substantially lessen competition. Second, market definition allows the Agencies to identify market participants and measure market shares and market concentration. See Section 5. The measurement of market shares and market concentration is not an end in itself, but is useful to the extent it illuminates the merger's likely competitive effects.

The Agencies' analysis need not start with market definition. Some of the analytical tools used by the Agencies to assess competitive effects do not rely on market definition, although evaluation of competitive alternatives available to customers is always necessary at some point in the analysis.

Evidence of competitive effects can inform market definition, just as market definition can be informative regarding competitive effects. For example, evidence that a reduction in the number of significant rivals offering a group of products causes prices for those products to rise significantly can itself establish that those products form a relevant market. Such evidence also may more directly predict the competitive effects of a merger, reducing the role of inferences from market definition and market shares.

Where analysis suggests alternative and reasonably plausible candidate markets, and where the resulting market shares lead to very different inferences regarding competitive effects, it is particularly valuable to examine more direct forms of evidence concerning those effects.

Market definition focuses solely on demand substitution factors, i.e., on customers' ability and willingness to substitute away from one product to another in response to a price increase or a corresponding non-price change such as a reduction in product quality or service. The responsive actions of suppliers are also important in competitive analysis. They are considered in these Guidelines in the sections addressing the identification of market participants, the measurement of market shares, the analysis of competitive effects, and entry.

Customers often confront a range of possible substitutes for the products of the merging firms. Some substitutes may be closer, and others more distant, either geographically or in terms of product attributes and perceptions. Additionally, customers may assess the proximity of different products differently. When products or suppliers in different geographic areas are substitutes for one another to varying degrees, defining a market to include some substitutes and exclude others is inevitably a simplification that cannot capture the full variation in the extent to which different products compete against each other. The principles of market definition outlined below seek to make this inevitable simplification as useful and informative as is practically possible. Relevant markets need not have precise metes and bounds.

Defining a market broadly to include relatively distant product or geographic substitutes can lead to misleading market shares. This is because the competitive significance of distant substitutes is unlikely to be commensurate with their shares in a broad market. Although excluding more distant substitutes from the market inevitably understates their competitive significance to some degree, doing so often provides a more accurate indicator of the competitive effects of the merger than would the alternative of including them and overstating their competitive significance as proportional to their shares in an expanded market.

> *Example 4:* Firms A and B, sellers of two leading brands of motorcycles, propose to merge. If Brand A motorcycle prices were to rise, some buyers would substitute to Brand B, and some others would substitute to cars. However, motorcycle buyers see Brand B motorcycles as much more similar to Brand A motorcycles than are cars. Far more cars are sold than motorcycles. Evaluating shares in a market that includes cars would greatly underestimate the competitive significance of Brand B motorcycles in constraining Brand A's prices and greatly overestimate the significance of cars.

Market shares of different products in narrowly defined markets are more likely to capture the relative competitive significance of these products, and often more accurately reflect competition between close substitutes. As a result, properly defined antitrust markets often exclude some substitutes to which some customers might turn in the face of a price increase even if such substitutes provide alternatives for those customers. However, a group of products is too narrow to constitute a relevant market if competition from products outside that group is so ample that even the complete elimination of competition within the group would not significantly harm either direct customers or downstream consumers. The hypothetical monopolist test (see Section 4.1.1) is designed to ensure that candidate markets are not overly narrow in this respect.

The Agencies implement these principles of market definition flexibly when evaluating different possible candidate markets. Relevant antitrust markets defined according to the hypothetical monopolist test are not always intuitive and may not align with how industry members use the term "market."

Section 4.1 describes the principles that apply to product market definition, and gives guidance on how the Agencies most often apply those principles. Section 4.2 describes how the same principles apply to geographic market definition. Although discussed separately for simplicity of exposition, the principles described in Sections 4.1 and 4.2 are combined to define a relevant market, which has both a product and a geographic dimension. In particular, the hypothetical monopolist test is applied to a group of products together with a geographic region to determine a relevant market.

4.1 Product Market Definition

When a product sold by one merging firm (Product A) competes against one or more products sold by the other merging firm, the Agencies define a relevant product market around Product A to evaluate the importance of that competition. Such a relevant product market consists of a group of substitute products including Product A. Multiple relevant product markets may thus be identified.

4.1.1 The Hypothetical Monopolist Test

The Agencies employ the hypothetical monopolist test to evaluate whether groups of products in candidate markets are sufficiently broad to constitute relevant antitrust markets. The Agencies use the hypothetical monopolist test to identify a set of products that are reasonably interchangeable with a product sold by one of the merging firms.

The hypothetical monopolist test requires that a product market contain enough substitute products so that it could be subject to post-merger exercise of market power significantly exceeding that existing absent the merger. Specifically, the test requires that a hypothetical profit-maximizing firm, not subject to price regulation, that was the only present and future seller of those products ("hypothetical monopolist") likely would impose at least a small but significant and non-transitory increase in price ("SSNIP") on at least one product in the market, including at least one product sold by one of the merging firms.[4] For the purpose of analyzing this issue, the terms of sale of products outside the candidate market are held constant. The SSNIP is employed solely as a methodological tool for performing the hypothetical monopolist test; it is not a tolerance level for price increases resulting from a merger.

Groups of products may satisfy the hypothetical monopolist test without including the full range of substitutes from which customers choose. The hypothetical monopolist test may identify a group of products as a relevant market even if customers would substitute significantly to products outside that group in response to a price increase.

> *Example 5:* Products A and B are being tested as a candidate market. Each sells for $100, has an incremental cost of $60, and sells 1200 units. For every dollar increase in the price of Product A, for any given price of Product B, Product A loses twenty units of sales to products outside the candidate market and ten units of sales to Product B, and likewise for Product B. Under these conditions, economic analysis shows that a hypothetical profit-maximizing monopolist controlling Products A and B would raise both of their prices by ten percent, to $110. Therefore, Products A and B satisfy the hypothetical monopolist test using a five percent SSNIP, and indeed for any SSNIP size up to ten percent. This is true even though two-thirds of the sales lost by one product when it raises its price are diverted to products outside the relevant market.

When applying the hypothetical monopolist test to define a market around a product offered by one of the merging firms, if the market includes a second product, the Agencies will normally also include a third product if that third product is a closer substitute for the first product than is the second product. The third product is a closer substitute if, in response to a SSNIP on the first product, greater revenues are diverted to the third product than to the second product.

> *Example 6:* In Example 5, suppose that half of the unit sales lost by Product A when it raises its price are diverted to Product C, which also has a price of $100, while one-third are diverted to Product B. Product C is a closer substitute for Product A than is Product B. Thus Product C will normally be included in the relevant market, even though Products A and B together satisfy the hypothetical monopolist test.

The hypothetical monopolist test ensures that markets are not defined too narrowly, but it does not lead to a single relevant market. The Agencies may evaluate a merger in any relevant market

---

[4] If the pricing incentives of the firms supplying the products in the candidate market differ substantially from those of the hypothetical monopolist, for reasons other than the latter's control over a larger group of substitutes, the Agencies may instead employ the concept of a hypothetical profit-maximizing cartel comprised of the firms (with all their products) that sell the products in the candidate market. This approach is most likely to be appropriate if the merging firms sell products outside the candidate market that significantly affect their pricing incentives for products in the candidate market. This could occur, for example, if the candidate market is one for durable equipment and the firms selling that equipment derive substantial net revenues from selling spare parts and service for that equipment.

satisfying the test, guided by the overarching principle that the purpose of defining the market and measuring market shares is to illuminate the evaluation of competitive effects. Because the relative competitive significance of more distant substitutes is apt to be overstated by their share of sales, when the Agencies rely on market shares and concentration, they usually do so in the smallest relevant market satisfying the hypothetical monopolist test.

> *Example 7:* In Example 4, including cars in the market will lead to misleadingly small market shares for motorcycle producers. Unless motorcycles fail the hypothetical monopolist test, the Agencies would not include cars in the market in analyzing this motorcycle merger.

4.1.2 Benchmark Prices and SSNIP Size

The Agencies apply the SSNIP starting from prices that would likely prevail absent the merger. If prices are not likely to change absent the merger, these benchmark prices can reasonably be taken to be the prices prevailing prior to the merger.[5] If prices are likely to change absent the merger, e.g., because of innovation or entry, the Agencies may use anticipated future prices as the benchmark for the test. If prices might fall absent the merger due to the breakdown of pre-merger coordination, the Agencies may use those lower prices as the benchmark for the test. In some cases, the techniques employed by the Agencies to implement the hypothetical monopolist test focus on the difference in incentives between pre-merger firms and the hypothetical monopolist and do not require specifying the benchmark prices.

The SSNIP is intended to represent a "small but significant" increase in the prices charged by firms in the candidate market for the value they contribute to the products or services used by customers. This properly directs attention to the effects of price changes commensurate with those that might result from a significant lessening of competition caused by the merger. This methodology is used because normally it is possible to quantify "small but significant" adverse price effects on customers and analyze their likely reactions, not because price effects are more important than non-price effects.

The Agencies most often use a SSNIP of five percent of the price paid by customers for the products or services to which the merging firms contribute value. However, what constitutes a "small but significant" increase in price, commensurate with a significant loss of competition caused by the merger, depends upon the nature of the industry and the merging firms' positions in it, and the Agencies may accordingly use a price increase that is larger or smaller than five percent. Where explicit or implicit prices for the firms' specific contribution to value can be identified with reasonable clarity, the Agencies may base the SSNIP on those prices.

> *Example 8:* In a merger between two oil pipelines, the SSNIP would be based on the price charged for transporting the oil, not on the price of the oil itself. If pipelines buy the oil at one end and sell it at the other, the price charged for transporting the oil is implicit, equal to the difference between the price paid for oil at the input end and the price charged for oil at the output end. The relevant product sold by the pipelines is better described as "pipeline transportation of oil from point A to point B" than as "oil at point B."

---

[5] Market definition for the evaluation of non-merger antitrust concerns such as monopolization or facilitating practices will differ in this respect if the effects resulting from the conduct of concern are already occurring at the time of evaluation.

Example 9: In a merger between two firms that install computers purchased from third parties, the SSNIP would be based on their fees, not on the price of installed computers. If these firms purchase the computers and charge their customers one package price, the implicit installation fee is equal to the package charge to customers less the price of the computers.

Example 10: In Example 9, suppose that the prices paid by the merging firms to purchase computers are opaque, but account for at least ninety-five percent of the prices they charge for installed computers, with profits or implicit fees making up five percent of those prices at most. A five percent SSNIP on the total price paid by customers would at least double those fees or profits. Even if that would be unprofitable for a hypothetical monopolist, a significant increase in fees might well be profitable. If the SSNIP is based on the total price paid by customers, a lower percentage will be used.

4.1.3 *Implementing the Hypothetical Monopolist Test*

The hypothetical monopolist's incentive to raise prices depends both on the extent to which customers would likely substitute away from the products in the candidate market in response to such a price increase and on the profit margins earned on those products. The profit margin on incremental units is the difference between price and incremental cost on those units. The Agencies often estimate incremental costs, for example using merging parties' documents or data the merging parties use to make business decisions. Incremental cost is measured over the change in output that would be caused by the price increase under consideration.

In considering customers' likely responses to higher prices, the Agencies take into account any reasonably available and reliable evidence, including, but not limited to:

- how customers have shifted purchases in the past in response to relative changes in price or other terms and conditions;

- information from buyers, including surveys, concerning how they would respond to price changes;

- the conduct of industry participants, notably:

  o sellers' business decisions or business documents indicating sellers' informed beliefs concerning how customers would substitute among products in response to relative changes in price;

  o industry participants' behavior in tracking and responding to price changes by some or all rivals;

- objective information about product characteristics and the costs and delays of switching products, especially switching from products in the candidate market to products outside the candidate market;

- the percentage of sales lost by one product in the candidate market, when its price alone rises, that is recaptured by other products in the candidate market, with a higher recapture percentage making a price increase more profitable for the hypothetical monopolist;

- evidence from other industry participants, such as sellers of complementary products;

- legal or regulatory requirements; and
- the influence of downstream competition faced by customers in their output markets.

When the necessary data are available, the Agencies also may consider a "critical loss analysis" to assess the extent to which it corroborates inferences drawn from the evidence noted above. Critical loss analysis asks whether imposing at least a SSNIP on one or more products in a candidate market would raise or lower the hypothetical monopolist's profits. While this "breakeven" analysis differs from the profit-maximizing analysis called for by the hypothetical monopolist test in Section 4.1.1, merging parties sometimes present this type of analysis to the Agencies. A price increase raises profits on sales made at the higher price, but this will be offset to the extent customers substitute away from products in the candidate market. Critical loss analysis compares the magnitude of these two offsetting effects resulting from the price increase. The "critical loss" is defined as the number of lost unit sales that would leave profits unchanged. The "predicted loss" is defined as the number of unit sales that the hypothetical monopolist is predicted to lose due to the price increase. The price increase raises the hypothetical monopolist's profits if the predicted loss is less than the critical loss.

The Agencies consider all of the evidence of customer substitution noted above in assessing the predicted loss. The Agencies require that estimates of the predicted loss be consistent with that evidence, including the pre-merger margins of products in the candidate market used to calculate the critical loss. Unless the firms are engaging in coordinated interaction (see Section 7), high pre-merger margins normally indicate that each firm's product individually faces demand that is not highly sensitive to price.[6] Higher pre-merger margins thus indicate a smaller predicted loss as well as a smaller critical loss. The higher the pre-merger margin, the smaller the recapture percentage necessary for the candidate market to satisfy the hypothetical monopolist test.

Even when the evidence necessary to perform the hypothetical monopolist test quantitatively is not available, the conceptual framework of the test provides a useful methodological tool for gathering and analyzing evidence pertinent to customer substitution and to market definition. The Agencies follow the hypothetical monopolist test to the extent possible given the available evidence, bearing in mind that the ultimate goal of market definition is to help determine whether the merger may substantially lessen competition.

4.1.4   Product Market Definition with Targeted Customers

If a hypothetical monopolist could profitably target a subset of customers for price increases, the Agencies may identify relevant markets defined around those targeted customers, to whom a hypothetical monopolist would profitably and separately impose at least a SSNIP. Markets to serve targeted customers are also known as price discrimination markets. In practice, the Agencies identify price discrimination markets only where they believe there is a realistic prospect of an adverse competitive effect on a group of targeted customers.

> *Example 11:* Glass containers have many uses. In response to a price increase for glass containers, some users would substitute substantially to plastic or metal containers, but baby food manufacturers would not. If a

---

[6] While margins are important for implementing the hypothetical monopolist test, high margins are not in themselves of antitrust concern.

hypothetical monopolist could price separately and limit arbitrage, baby food manufacturers would be vulnerable to a targeted increase in the price of glass containers. The Agencies could define a distinct market for glass containers used to package baby food.

The Agencies also often consider markets for targeted customers when prices are individually negotiated and suppliers have information about customers that would allow a hypothetical monopolist to identify customers that are likely to pay a higher price for the relevant product. If prices are negotiated individually with customers, the hypothetical monopolist test may suggest relevant markets that are as narrow as individual customers (see also Section 6.2 on bargaining and auctions). Nonetheless, the Agencies often define markets for groups of targeted customers, i.e., by type of customer, rather than by individual customer. By so doing, the Agencies are able to rely on aggregated market shares that can be more helpful in predicting the competitive effects of the merger.

4.2 Geographic Market Definition

The arena of competition affected by the merger may be geographically bounded if geography limits some customers' willingness or ability to substitute to some products, or some suppliers' willingness or ability to serve some customers. Both supplier and customer locations can affect this. The Agencies apply the principles of market definition described here and in Section 4.1 to define a relevant market with a geographic dimension as well as a product dimension.

The scope of geographic markets often depends on transportation costs. Other factors such as language, regulation, tariff and non-tariff trade barriers, custom and familiarity, reputation, and service availability may impede long-distance or international transactions. The competitive significance of foreign firms may be assessed at various exchange rates, especially if exchange rates have fluctuated in the recent past.

In the absence of price discrimination based on customer location, the Agencies normally define geographic markets based on the locations of suppliers, as explained in subsection 4.2.1. In other cases, notably if price discrimination based on customer location is feasible as is often the case when delivered pricing is commonly used in the industry, the Agencies may define geographic markets based on the locations of customers, as explained in subsection 4.2.2.

4.2.1 *Geographic Markets Based on the Locations of Suppliers*

Geographic markets based on the locations of suppliers encompass the region from which sales are made. Geographic markets of this type often apply when customers receive goods or services at suppliers' locations. Competitors in the market are firms with relevant production, sales, or service facilities in that region. Some customers who buy from these firms may be located outside the boundaries of the geographic market.

The hypothetical monopolist test requires that a hypothetical profit-maximizing firm that was the only present or future producer of the relevant product(s) located in the region would impose at least a SSNIP from at least one location, including at least one location of one of the merging firms. In this exercise the terms of sale for all products produced elsewhere are held constant. A single firm may operate in a number of different geographic markets, even for a single product.

Example 12: The merging parties both have manufacturing plants in City X. The relevant product is expensive to transport and suppliers price their products for pickup at their locations. Rival plants are some distance away in City Y. A hypothetical monopolist controlling all plants in City X could profitably impose a SSNIP at these plants. Competition from more distant plants would not defeat the price increase because supplies coming from more distant plants require expensive transportation. The relevant geographic market is defined around the plants in City X.

When the geographic market is defined based on supplier locations, sales made by suppliers located in the geographic market are counted, regardless of the location of the customer making the purchase.

In considering likely reactions of customers to price increases for the relevant product(s) imposed in a candidate geographic market, the Agencies consider any reasonably available and reliable evidence, including:

- how customers have shifted purchases in the past between different geographic locations in response to relative changes in price or other terms and conditions;

- the cost and difficulty of transporting the product (or the cost and difficulty of a customer traveling to a seller's location), in relation to its price;

- whether suppliers need a presence near customers to provide service or support;

- evidence on whether sellers base business decisions on the prospect of customers switching between geographic locations in response to relative changes in price or other competitive variables;

- the costs and delays of switching from suppliers in the candidate geographic market to suppliers outside the candidate geographic market; and

- the influence of downstream competition faced by customers in their output markets.

4.2.2   Geographic Markets Based on the Locations of Customers

When the hypothetical monopolist could discriminate based on customer location, the Agencies may define geographic markets based on the locations of targeted customers.[7] Geographic markets of this type often apply when suppliers deliver their products or services to customers' locations. Geographic markets of this type encompass the region into which sales are made. Competitors in the market are firms that sell to customers in the specified region. Some suppliers that sell into the relevant market may be located outside the boundaries of the geographic market.

The hypothetical monopolist test requires that a hypothetical profit-maximizing firm that was the only present or future seller of the relevant product(s) to customers in the region would impose at least a SSNIP on some customers in that region. A region forms a relevant geographic market if this price increase would not be defeated by substitution away from the relevant product or by arbitrage,

---

[7] For customers operating in multiple locations, only those customer locations within the targeted zone are included in the market.

e.g., customers in the region travelling outside it to purchase the relevant product. In this exercise, the terms of sale for products sold to all customers outside the region are held constant.

> *Example 13:* Customers require local sales and support. Suppliers have sales and service operations in many geographic areas and can discriminate based on customer location. The geographic market can be defined around the locations of customers.
>
> *Example 14:* Each merging firm has a single manufacturing plant and delivers the relevant product to customers in City X and in City Y. The relevant product is expensive to transport. The merging firms' plants are by far the closest to City X, but no closer to City Y than are numerous rival plants. This fact pattern suggests that customers in City X may be harmed by the merger even if customers in City Y are not. For that reason, the Agencies consider a relevant geographic market defined around customers in City X. Such a market could be defined even if the region around the merging firms' plants would not be a relevant geographic market defined based on the location of sellers because a hypothetical monopolist controlling all plants in that region would find a SSNIP imposed on all of its customers unprofitable due to the loss of sales to customers in City Y.

When the geographic market is defined based on customer locations, sales made to those customers are counted, regardless of the location of the supplier making those sales.

> *Example 15:* Customers in the United States must use products approved by U.S. regulators. Foreign customers use products not approved by U.S. regulators. The relevant product market consists of products approved by U.S. regulators. The geographic market is defined around U.S. customers. Any sales made to U.S. customers by foreign suppliers are included in the market, and those foreign suppliers are participants in the U.S. market even though located outside it.

5. Market Participants, Market Shares, and Market Concentration

The Agencies normally consider measures of market shares and market concentration as part of their evaluation of competitive effects. The Agencies evaluate market shares and concentration in conjunction with other reasonably available and reliable evidence for the ultimate purpose of determining whether a merger may substantially lessen competition.

Market shares can directly influence firms' competitive incentives. For example, if a price reduction to gain new customers would also apply to a firm's existing customers, a firm with a large market share may be more reluctant to implement a price reduction than one with a small share. Likewise, a firm with a large market share may not feel pressure to reduce price even if a smaller rival does. Market shares also can reflect firms' capabilities. For example, a firm with a large market share may be able to expand output rapidly by a larger absolute amount than can a small firm. Similarly, a large market share tends to indicate low costs, an attractive product, or both.

5.1 Market Participants

All firms that currently earn revenues in the relevant market are considered market participants. Vertically integrated firms are also included to the extent that their inclusion accurately reflects their competitive significance. Firms not currently earning revenues in the relevant market, but that have committed to entering the market in the near future, are also considered market participants.

Firms that are not current producers in a relevant market, but that would very likely provide rapid supply responses with direct competitive impact in the event of a SSNIP, without incurring significant sunk costs, are also considered market participants. These firms are termed "rapid entrants." Sunk costs are entry or exit costs that cannot be recovered outside the relevant market. Entry that would take place more slowly in response to adverse competitive effects, or that requires firms to incur significant sunk costs, is considered in Section 9.

Firms that produce the relevant product but do not sell it in the relevant geographic market may be rapid entrants. Other things equal, such firms are most likely to be rapid entrants if they are close to the geographic market.

> *Example 16:* Farm A grows tomatoes halfway between Cities X and Y. Currently, it ships its tomatoes to City X because prices there are two percent higher. Previously it has varied the destination of its shipments in response to small price variations. Farm A would likely be a rapid entrant participant in a market for tomatoes in City Y.
>
> *Example 17:* Firm B has bid multiple times to supply milk to School District S, and actually supplies milk to schools in some adjacent areas. It has never won a bid in School District S, but is well qualified to serve that district and has often nearly won. Firm B would be counted as a rapid entrant in a market for school milk in School District S.

More generally, if the relevant market is defined around targeted customers, firms that produce relevant products but do not sell them to those customers may be rapid entrants if they can easily and rapidly begin selling to the targeted customers.

Firms that clearly possess the necessary assets to supply into the relevant market rapidly may also be rapid entrants. In markets for relatively homogeneous goods where a supplier's ability to compete depends predominantly on its costs and its capacity, and not on other factors such as experience or reputation in the relevant market, a supplier with efficient idle capacity, or readily available "swing" capacity currently used in adjacent markets that can easily and profitably be shifted to serve the relevant market, may be a rapid entrant.[8] However, idle capacity may be inefficient, and capacity used in adjacent markets may not be available, so a firm's possession of idle or swing capacity alone does not make that firm a rapid entrant.

5.2   Market Shares

The Agencies normally calculate market shares for all firms that currently produce products in the relevant market, subject to the availability of data. The Agencies also calculate market shares for other market participants if this can be done to reliably reflect their competitive significance.

Market concentration and market share data are normally based on historical evidence. However, recent or ongoing changes in market conditions may indicate that the current market share of a particular firm either understates or overstates the firm's future competitive significance. The Agencies consider reasonably predictable effects of recent or ongoing changes in market conditions when calculating and interpreting market share data. For example, if a new technology that is important to long-term competitive viability is available to other firms in the market, but is not available to a particular firm, the Agencies may conclude that that firm's historical market share

---

[8] If this type of supply side substitution is nearly universal among the firms selling one or more of a group of products, the Agencies may use an aggregate description of markets for those products as a matter of convenience.

overstates its future competitive significance. The Agencies may project historical market shares into the foreseeable future when this can be done reliably.

The Agencies measure market shares based on the best available indicator of firms' future competitive significance in the relevant market. This may depend upon the type of competitive effect being considered, and on the availability of data. Typically, annual data are used, but where individual transactions are large and infrequent so annual data may be unrepresentative, the Agencies may measure market shares over a longer period of time.

In most contexts, the Agencies measure each firm's market share based on its actual or projected revenues in the relevant market. Revenues in the relevant market tend to be the best measure of attractiveness to customers, since they reflect the real-world ability of firms to surmount all of the obstacles necessary to offer products on terms and conditions that are attractive to customers. In cases where one unit of a low-priced product can substitute for one unit of a higher-priced product, unit sales may measure competitive significance better than revenues. For example, a new, much less expensive product may have great competitive significance if it substantially erodes the revenues earned by older, higher-priced products, even if it earns relatively few revenues. In cases where customers sign long-term contracts, face switching costs, or tend to re-evaluate their suppliers only occasionally, revenues earned from recently acquired customers may better reflect the competitive significance of suppliers than do total revenues.

In markets for homogeneous products, a firm's competitive significance may derive principally from its ability and incentive to rapidly expand production in the relevant market in response to a price increase or output reduction by others in that market. As a result, a firm's competitive significance may depend upon its level of readily available capacity to serve the relevant market if that capacity is efficient enough to make such expansion profitable. In such markets, capacities or reserves may better reflect the future competitive significance of suppliers than revenues, and the Agencies may calculate market shares using those measures. Market participants that are not current producers may then be assigned positive market shares, but only if a measure of their competitive significance properly comparable to that of current producers is available. When market shares are measured based on firms' readily available capacities, the Agencies do not include capacity that is committed or so profitably employed outside the relevant market, or so high-cost, that it would not likely be used to respond to a SSNIP in the relevant market.

> *Example 18:* The geographic market is defined around customers in the United States. Firm X produces the relevant product outside the United States, and most of its sales are made to customers outside the United States. In most contexts, Firm X's market share will be based on its sales to U.S. customers, not its total sales or total capacity. However, if the relevant product is homogeneous, and if Firm X would significantly expand sales to U.S. customers rapidly and without incurring significant sunk costs in response to a SSNIP, the Agencies may base Firm X's market share on its readily available capacity to serve U.S. customers.

When the Agencies define markets serving targeted customers, these same principles are used to measure market shares, as they apply to those customers. In most contexts, each firm's market share is based on its actual or projected revenues from the targeted customers. However, the Agencies may instead measure market shares based on revenues from a broader group of customers if doing so would more accurately reflect the competitive significance of different suppliers in the relevant market. Revenues earned from a broader group of customers may also be used when better data are thereby available.

5.3 Market Concentration

Market concentration is often one useful indicator of likely competitive effects of a merger. In evaluating market concentration, the Agencies consider both the post-merger level of market concentration and the change in concentration resulting from a merger. Market shares may not fully reflect the competitive significance of firms in the market or the impact of a merger. They are used in conjunction with other evidence of competitive effects. See Sections 6 and 7.

In analyzing mergers between an incumbent and a recent or potential entrant, to the extent the Agencies use the change in concentration to evaluate competitive effects, they will do so using projected market shares. A merger between an incumbent and a potential entrant can raise significant competitive concerns. The lessening of competition resulting from such a merger is more likely to be substantial, the larger is the market share of the incumbent, the greater is the competitive significance of the potential entrant, and the greater is the competitive threat posed by this potential entrant relative to others.

The Agencies give more weight to market concentration when market shares have been stable over time, especially in the face of historical changes in relative prices or costs. If a firm has retained its market share even after its price has increased relative to those of its rivals, that firm already faces limited competitive constraints, making it less likely that its remaining rivals will replace the competition lost if one of that firm's important rivals is eliminated due to a merger. By contrast, even a highly concentrated market can be very competitive if market shares fluctuate substantially over short periods of time in response to changes in competitive offerings. However, if competition by one of the merging firms has significantly contributed to these fluctuations, perhaps because it has acted as a maverick, the Agencies will consider whether the merger will enhance market power by combining that firm with one of its significant rivals.

The Agencies may measure market concentration using the number of significant competitors in the market. This measure is most useful when there is a gap in market share between significant competitors and smaller rivals or when it is difficult to measure revenues in the relevant market. The Agencies also may consider the combined market share of the merging firms as an indicator of the extent to which others in the market may not be able readily to replace competition between the merging firms that is lost through the merger.

The Agencies often calculate the Herfindahl-Hirschman Index ("HHI") of market concentration. The HHI is calculated by summing the squares of the individual firms' market shares,[9] and thus gives proportionately greater weight to the larger market shares. When using the HHI, the Agencies

---

[9] For example, a market consisting of four firms with market shares of thirty percent, thirty percent, twenty percent, and twenty percent has an HHI of 2600 ($30^2 + 30^2 + 20^2 + 20^2 = 2600$). The HHI ranges from 10,000 (in the case of a pure monopoly) to a number approaching zero (in the case of an atomistic market). Although it is desirable to include all firms in the calculation, lack of information about firms with small shares is not critical because such firms do not affect the HHI significantly.

consider both the post-merger level of the HHI and the increase in the HHI resulting from the merger. The increase in the HHI is equal to twice the product of the market shares of the merging firms.[10]

Based on their experience, the Agencies generally classify markets into three types:

- Unconcentrated Markets: HHI below 1500

- Moderately Concentrated Markets: HHI between 1500 and 2500

- Highly Concentrated Markets: HHI above 2500

The Agencies employ the following general standards for the relevant markets they have defined:

- *Small Change in Concentration:* Mergers involving an increase in the HHI of less than 100 points are unlikely to have adverse competitive effects and ordinarily require no further analysis.

- *Unconcentrated Markets:* Mergers resulting in unconcentrated markets are unlikely to have adverse competitive effects and ordinarily require no further analysis.

- *Moderately Concentrated Markets:* Mergers resulting in moderately concentrated markets that involve an increase in the HHI of more than 100 points potentially raise significant competitive concerns and often warrant scrutiny.

- *Highly Concentrated Markets:* Mergers resulting in highly concentrated markets that involve an increase in the HHI of between 100 points and 200 points potentially raise significant competitive concerns and often warrant scrutiny. Mergers resulting in highly concentrated markets that involve an increase in the HHI of more than 200 points will be presumed to be likely to enhance market power. The presumption may be rebutted by persuasive evidence showing that the merger is unlikely to enhance market power.

The purpose of these thresholds is not to provide a rigid screen to separate competitively benign mergers from anticompetitive ones, although high levels of concentration do raise concerns. Rather, they provide one way to identify some mergers unlikely to raise competitive concerns and some others for which it is particularly important to examine whether other competitive factors confirm, reinforce, or counteract the potentially harmful effects of increased concentration. The higher the post-merger HHI and the increase in the HHI, the greater are the Agencies' potential competitive concerns and the greater is the likelihood that the Agencies will request additional information to conduct their analysis.

---

[10] For example, the merger of firms with shares of five percent and ten percent of the market would increase the HHI by 100 ($5 \times 10 \times 2 = 100$).

6. Unilateral Effects

The elimination of competition between two firms that results from their merger may alone constitute a substantial lessening of competition. Such unilateral effects are most apparent in a merger to monopoly in a relevant market, but are by no means limited to that case. Whether cognizable efficiencies resulting from the merger are likely to reduce or reverse adverse unilateral effects is addressed in Section 10.

Several common types of unilateral effects are discussed in this section. Section 6.1 discusses unilateral price effects in markets with differentiated products. Section 6.2 discusses unilateral effects in markets where sellers negotiate with buyers or prices are determined through auctions. Section 6.3 discusses unilateral effects relating to reductions in output or capacity in markets for relatively homogeneous products. Section 6.4 discusses unilateral effects arising from diminished innovation or reduced product variety. These effects do not exhaust the types of possible unilateral effects; for example, exclusionary unilateral effects also can arise.

A merger may result in different unilateral effects along different dimensions of competition. For example, a merger may increase prices in the short term but not raise longer-term concerns about innovation, either because rivals will provide sufficient innovation competition or because the merger will generate cognizable research and development efficiencies. See Section 10.

6.1 Pricing of Differentiated Products

In differentiated product industries, some products can be very close substitutes and compete strongly with each other, while other products are more distant substitutes and compete less strongly. For example, one high-end product may compete much more directly with another high-end product than with any low-end product.

A merger between firms selling differentiated products may diminish competition by enabling the merged firm to profit by unilaterally raising the price of one or both products above the pre-merger level. Some of the sales lost due to the price rise will merely be diverted to the product of the merger partner and, depending on relative margins, capturing such sales loss through merger may make the price increase profitable even though it would not have been profitable prior to the merger.

The extent of direct competition between the products sold by the merging parties is central to the evaluation of unilateral price effects. Unilateral price effects are greater, the more the buyers of products sold by one merging firm consider products sold by the other merging firm to be their next choice. The Agencies consider any reasonably available and reliable information to evaluate the extent of direct competition between the products sold by the merging firms. This includes documentary and testimonial evidence, win/loss reports and evidence from discount approval processes, customer switching patterns, and customer surveys. The types of evidence relied on often overlap substantially with the types of evidence of customer substitution relevant to the hypothetical monopolist test. See Section 4.1.1.

Substantial unilateral price elevation post-merger for a product formerly sold by one of the merging firms normally requires that a significant fraction of the customers purchasing that product view products formerly sold by the other merging firm as their next-best choice. However, unless pre-merger margins between price and incremental cost are low, that significant fraction need not approach a majority. For this purpose, incremental cost is measured over the change in output that would be caused by the price change considered. A merger may produce significant unilateral effects for a given product even though many more sales are diverted to products sold by non-merging firms than to products previously sold by the merger partner.

> *Example 19:* In Example 5, the merged entity controlling Products A and B would raise prices ten percent, given the product offerings and prices of other firms. In that example, one-third of the sales lost by Product A when its price alone is raised are diverted to Product B. Further analysis is required to account for repositioning, entry, and efficiencies.

In some cases, the Agencies may seek to quantify the extent of direct competition between a product sold by one merging firm and a second product sold by the other merging firm by estimating the diversion ratio from the first product to the second product. The diversion ratio is the fraction of unit sales lost by the first product due to an increase in its price that would be diverted to the second product. Diversion ratios between products sold by one merging firm and products sold by the other merging firm can be very informative for assessing unilateral price effects, with higher diversion ratios indicating a greater likelihood of such effects. Diversion ratios between products sold by merging firms and those sold by non-merging firms have at most secondary predictive value.

Adverse unilateral price effects can arise when the merger gives the merged entity an incentive to raise the price of a product previously sold by one merging firm and thereby divert sales to products previously sold by the other merging firm, boosting the profits on the latter products. Taking as given other prices and product offerings, that boost to profits is equal to the value to the merged firm of the sales diverted to those products. The value of sales diverted to a product is equal to the number of units diverted to that product multiplied by the margin between price and incremental cost on that product. In some cases, where sufficient information is available, the Agencies assess the value of diverted sales, which can serve as an indicator of the upward pricing pressure on the first product resulting from the merger. Diagnosing unilateral price effects based on the value of diverted sales need not rely on market definition or the calculation of market shares and concentration. The Agencies rely much more on the value of diverted sales than on the level of the HHI for diagnosing unilateral price effects in markets with differentiated products. If the value of diverted sales is proportionately small, significant unilateral price effects are unlikely.[11]

Where sufficient data are available, the Agencies may construct economic models designed to quantify the unilateral price effects resulting from the merger. These models often include independent price responses by non-merging firms. They also can incorporate merger-specific efficiencies. These merger simulation methods need not rely on market definition. The Agencies do not treat merger simulation evidence as conclusive in itself, and they place more weight on whether their merger simulations consistently predict substantial price increases than on the precise prediction of any single simulation.

---

[11] For this purpose, the value of diverted sales is measured in proportion to the lost revenues attributable to the reduction in unit sales resulting from the price increase. Those lost revenues equal the reduction in the number of units sold of that product multiplied by that product's price.

A merger is unlikely to generate substantial unilateral price increases if non-merging parties offer very close substitutes for the products offered by the merging firms. In some cases, non-merging firms may be able to reposition their products to offer close substitutes for the products offered by the merging firms. Repositioning is a supply-side response that is evaluated much like entry, with consideration given to timeliness, likelihood, and sufficiency. See Section 9. The Agencies consider whether repositioning would be sufficient to deter or counteract what otherwise would be significant anticompetitive unilateral effects from a differentiated products merger.

6.2 Bargaining and Auctions

In many industries, especially those involving intermediate goods and services, buyers and sellers negotiate to determine prices and other terms of trade. In that process, buyers commonly negotiate with more than one seller, and may play sellers off against one another. Some highly structured forms of such competition are known as auctions. Negotiations often combine aspects of an auction with aspects of one-on-one negotiation, although pure auctions are sometimes used in government procurement and elsewhere.

A merger between two competing sellers prevents buyers from playing those sellers off against each other in negotiations. This alone can significantly enhance the ability and incentive of the merged entity to obtain a result more favorable to it, and less favorable to the buyer, than the merging firms would have offered separately absent the merger. The Agencies analyze unilateral effects of this type using similar approaches to those described in Section 6.1.

Anticompetitive unilateral effects in these settings are likely in proportion to the frequency or probability with which, prior to the merger, one of the merging sellers had been the runner-up when the other won the business. These effects also are likely to be greater, the greater advantage the runner-up merging firm has over other suppliers in meeting customers' needs. These effects also tend to be greater, the more profitable were the pre-merger winning bids. All of these factors are likely to be small if there are many equally placed bidders.

The mechanisms of these anticompetitive unilateral effects, and the indicia of their likelihood, differ somewhat according to the bargaining practices used, the auction format, and the sellers' information about one another's costs and about buyers' preferences. For example, when the merging sellers are likely to know which buyers they are best and second best placed to serve, any anticompetitive unilateral effects are apt to be targeted at those buyers; when sellers are less well informed, such effects are more apt to be spread over a broader class of buyers.

6.3 Capacity and Output for Homogeneous Products

In markets involving relatively undifferentiated products, the Agencies may evaluate whether the merged firm will find it profitable unilaterally to suppress output and elevate the market price. A firm may leave capacity idle, refrain from building or obtaining capacity that would have been obtained absent the merger, or eliminate pre-existing production capabilities. A firm may also divert the use of capacity away from one relevant market and into another so as to raise the price in the former market. The competitive analyses of these alternative modes of output suppression may differ.

A unilateral output suppression strategy is more likely to be profitable when (1) the merged firm's market share is relatively high; (2) the share of the merged firm's output already committed for sale at prices unaffected by the output suppression is relatively low; (3) the margin on the suppressed output is relatively low; (4) the supply responses of rivals are relatively small; and (5) the market elasticity of demand is relatively low.

A merger may provide the merged firm a larger base of sales on which to benefit from the resulting price rise, or it may eliminate a competitor that otherwise could have expanded its output in response to the price rise.

> *Example 20:* Firms A and B both produce an industrial commodity and propose to merge. The demand for this commodity is insensitive to price. Firm A is the market leader. Firm B produces substantial output, but its operating margins are low because it operates high-cost plants. The other suppliers are operating very near capacity. The merged firm has an incentive to reduce output at the high-cost plants, perhaps shutting down some of that capacity, thus driving up the price it receives on the remainder of its output. The merger harms customers, notwithstanding that the merged firm shifts some output from high-cost plants to low-cost plants.

In some cases, a merger between a firm with a substantial share of the sales in the market and a firm with significant excess capacity to serve that market can make an output suppression strategy profitable.[12] This can occur even if the firm with the excess capacity has a relatively small share of sales, if that firm's ability to expand, and thus keep price from rising, has been making an output suppression strategy unprofitable for the firm with the larger market share.

6.4 Innovation and Product Variety

Competition often spurs firms to innovate. The Agencies may consider whether a merger is likely to diminish innovation competition by encouraging the merged firm to curtail its innovative efforts below the level that would prevail in the absence of the merger. That curtailment of innovation could take the form of reduced incentive to continue with an existing product-development effort or reduced incentive to initiate development of new products.

The first of these effects is most likely to occur if at least one of the merging firms is engaging in efforts to introduce new products that would capture substantial revenues from the other merging firm. The second, longer-run effect is most likely to occur if at least one of the merging firms has capabilities that are likely to lead it to develop new products in the future that would capture substantial revenues from the other merging firm. The Agencies therefore also consider whether a merger will diminish innovation competition by combining two of a very small number of firms with the strongest capabilities to successfully innovate in a specific direction.

The Agencies evaluate the extent to which successful innovation by one merging firm is likely to take sales from the other, and the extent to which post-merger incentives for future innovation will be lower than those that would prevail in the absence of the merger. The Agencies also consider whether the merger is likely to enable innovation that would not otherwise take place, by bringing together

---

[12] Such a merger also can cause adverse coordinated effects, especially if the acquired firm with excess capacity was disrupting effective coordination.

complementary capabilities that cannot be otherwise combined or for some other merger-specific reason. See Section 10.

The Agencies also consider whether a merger is likely to give the merged firm an incentive to cease offering one of the relevant products sold by the merging parties. Reductions in variety following a merger may or may not be anticompetitive. Mergers can lead to the efficient consolidation of products when variety offers little in value to customers. In other cases, a merger may increase variety by encouraging the merged firm to reposition its products to be more differentiated from one another.

If the merged firm would withdraw a product that a significant number of customers strongly prefer to those products that would remain available, this can constitute a harm to customers over and above any effects on the price or quality of any given product. If there is evidence of such an effect, the Agencies may inquire whether the reduction in variety is largely due to a loss of competitive incentives attributable to the merger. An anticompetitive incentive to eliminate a product as a result of the merger is greater and more likely, the larger is the share of profits from that product coming at the expense of profits from products sold by the merger partner. Where a merger substantially reduces competition by bringing two close substitute products under common ownership, and one of those products is eliminated, the merger will often also lead to a price increase on the remaining product, but that is not a necessary condition for anticompetitive effect.

> *Example 21:* Firm A sells a high-end product at a premium price. Firm B sells a mid-range product at a lower price, serving customers who are more price sensitive. Several other firms have low-end products. Firms A and B together have a large share of the relevant market. Firm A proposes to acquire Firm B and discontinue Firm B's product. Firm A expects to retain most of Firm B's customers. Firm A may not find it profitable to raise the price of its high-end product after the merger, because doing so would reduce its ability to retain Firm B's more price-sensitive customers. The Agencies may conclude that the withdrawal of Firm B's product results from a loss of competition and materially harms customers.

7. Coordinated Effects

A merger may diminish competition by enabling or encouraging post-merger coordinated interaction among firms in the relevant market that harms customers. Coordinated interaction involves conduct by multiple firms that is profitable for each of them only as a result of the accommodating reactions of the others. These reactions can blunt a firm's incentive to offer customers better deals by undercutting the extent to which such a move would win business away from rivals. They also can enhance a firm's incentive to raise prices, by assuaging the fear that such a move would lose customers to rivals.

Coordinated interaction includes a range of conduct. Coordinated interaction can involve the explicit negotiation of a common understanding of how firms will compete or refrain from competing. Such conduct typically would itself violate the antitrust laws. Coordinated interaction also can involve a similar common understanding that is not explicitly negotiated but would be enforced by the detection and punishment of deviations that would undermine the coordinated interaction. Coordinated interaction alternatively can involve parallel accommodating conduct not pursuant to a prior understanding. Parallel accommodating conduct includes situations in which each rival's response to competitive moves made by others is individually rational, and not motivated by retaliation or deterrence nor intended to sustain an agreed-upon market outcome, but nevertheless emboldens price increases and weakens competitive incentives to reduce prices or offer customers better terms. Coordinated interaction includes conduct not otherwise condemned by the antitrust laws.

The ability of rival firms to engage in coordinated conduct depends on the strength and predictability of rivals' responses to a price change or other competitive initiative. Under some circumstances, a merger can result in market concentration sufficient to strengthen such responses or enable multiple firms in the market to predict them more confidently, thereby affecting the competitive incentives of multiple firms in the market, not just the merged firm.

7.1   Impact of Merger on Coordinated Interaction

The Agencies examine whether a merger is likely to change the manner in which market participants interact, inducing substantially more coordinated interaction. The Agencies seek to identify how a merger might significantly weaken competitive incentives through an increase in the strength, extent, or likelihood of coordinated conduct. There are, however, numerous forms of coordination, and the risk that a merger will induce adverse coordinated effects may not be susceptible to quantification or detailed proof. Therefore, the Agencies evaluate the risk of coordinated effects using measures of market concentration (see Section 5) in conjunction with an assessment of whether a market is vulnerable to coordinated conduct. See Section 7.2. The analysis in Section 7.2 applies to moderately and highly concentrated markets, as unconcentrated markets are unlikely to be vulnerable to coordinated conduct.

Pursuant to the Clayton Act's incipiency standard, the Agencies may challenge mergers that in their judgment pose a real danger of harm through coordinated effects, even without specific evidence showing precisely how the coordination likely would take place. The Agencies are likely to challenge a merger if the following three conditions are all met: (1) the merger would significantly increase concentration and lead to a moderately or highly concentrated market; (2) that market shows signs of vulnerability to coordinated conduct (see Section 7.2); and (3) the Agencies have a credible basis on which to conclude that the merger may enhance that vulnerability. An acquisition eliminating a maverick firm (see Section 2.1.5) in a market vulnerable to coordinated conduct is likely to cause adverse coordinated effects.

7.2   Evidence a Market is Vulnerable to Coordinated Conduct

The Agencies presume that market conditions are conducive to coordinated interaction if firms representing a substantial share in the relevant market appear to have previously engaged in express collusion affecting the relevant market, unless competitive conditions in the market have since changed significantly. Previous express collusion in another geographic market will have the same weight if the salient characteristics of that other market at the time of the collusion are comparable to those in the relevant market. Failed previous attempts at collusion in the relevant market suggest that successful collusion was difficult pre-merger but not so difficult as to deter attempts, and a merger may tend to make success more likely. Previous collusion or attempted collusion in another product market may also be given substantial weight if the salient characteristics of that other market at the time of the collusion are closely comparable to those in the relevant market.

A market typically is more vulnerable to coordinated conduct if each competitively important firm's significant competitive initiatives can be promptly and confidently observed by that firm's rivals. This is more likely to be the case if the terms offered to customers are relatively transparent. Price transparency can be greater for relatively homogeneous products. Even if terms of dealing are not transparent, transparency regarding the identities of the firms serving particular customers can give rise to coordination, e.g., through customer or territorial allocation. Regular monitoring by suppliers of one another's prices or customers can indicate that the terms offered to customers are relatively transparent.

A market typically is more vulnerable to coordinated conduct if a firm's prospective competitive reward from attracting customers away from its rivals will be significantly diminished by likely responses of those rivals. This is more likely to be the case, the stronger and faster are the responses the firm anticipates from its rivals. The firm is more likely to anticipate strong responses if there are few significant competitors, if products in the relevant market are relatively homogeneous, if customers find it relatively easy to switch between suppliers, or if suppliers use meeting-competition clauses.

A firm is more likely to be deterred from making competitive initiatives by whatever responses occur if sales are small and frequent rather than via occasional large and long-term contracts or if relatively few customers will switch to it before rivals are able to respond. A firm is less likely to be deterred by whatever responses occur if the firm has little stake in the status quo. For example, a firm with a small market share that can quickly and dramatically expand, constrained neither by limits on production nor by customer reluctance to switch providers or to entrust business to a historically small provider, is unlikely to be deterred. Firms are also less likely to be deterred by whatever responses occur if competition in the relevant market is marked by leapfrogging technological innovation, so that responses by competitors leave the gains from successful innovation largely intact.

A market is more apt to be vulnerable to coordinated conduct if the firm initiating a price increase will lose relatively few customers after rivals respond to the increase. Similarly, a market is more apt to be vulnerable to coordinated conduct if a firm that first offers a lower price or improved product to customers will retain relatively few customers thus attracted away from its rivals after those rivals respond.

The Agencies regard coordinated interaction as more likely, the more the participants stand to gain from successful coordination. Coordination generally is more profitable, the lower is the market elasticity of demand.

Coordinated conduct can harm customers even if not all firms in the relevant market engage in the coordination, but significant harm normally is likely only if a substantial part of the market is subject to such conduct. The prospect of harm depends on the collective market power, in the relevant market, of firms whose incentives to compete are substantially weakened by coordinated conduct. This collective market power is greater, the lower is the market elasticity of demand. This collective market power is diminished by the presence of other market participants with small market shares and little stake in the outcome resulting from the coordinated conduct, if these firms can rapidly expand their sales in the relevant market.

Buyer characteristics and the nature of the procurement process can affect coordination. For example, sellers may have the incentive to bid aggressively for a large contract even if they expect strong responses by rivals. This is especially the case for sellers with small market shares, if they can realistically win such large contracts. In some cases, a large buyer may be able to strategically undermine coordinated conduct, at least as it pertains to that buyer's needs, by choosing to put up for bid a few large contracts rather than many smaller ones, and by making its procurement decisions opaque to suppliers.

8. Powerful Buyers

Powerful buyers are often able to negotiate favorable terms with their suppliers. Such terms may reflect the lower costs of serving these buyers, but they also can reflect price discrimination in their favor.

The Agencies consider the possibility that powerful buyers may constrain the ability of the merging parties to raise prices. This can occur, for example, if powerful buyers have the ability and incentive to vertically integrate upstream or sponsor entry, or if the conduct or presence of large buyers undermines coordinated effects. However, the Agencies do not presume that the presence of powerful buyers alone forestalls adverse competitive effects flowing from the merger. Even buyers that can negotiate favorable terms may be harmed by an increase in market power. The Agencies examine the choices available to powerful buyers and how those choices likely would change due to the merger. Normally, a merger that eliminates a supplier whose presence contributed significantly to a buyer's negotiating leverage will harm that buyer.

> *Example 22:* Customer C has been able to negotiate lower pre-merger prices than other customers by threatening to shift its large volume of purchases from one merging firm to the other. No other suppliers are as well placed to meet Customer C's needs for volume and reliability. The merger is likely to harm Customer C. In this situation, the Agencies could identify a price discrimination market consisting of Customer C and similarly placed customers. The merger threatens to end previous price discrimination in their favor.

Furthermore, even if some powerful buyers could protect themselves, the Agencies also consider whether market power can be exercised against other buyers.

> *Example 23:* In Example 22, if Customer C instead obtained the lower pre-merger prices based on a credible threat to supply its own needs, or to sponsor new entry, Customer C might not be harmed. However, even in this case, other customers may still be harmed.

9. Entry

The analysis of competitive effects in Sections 6 and 7 focuses on current participants in the relevant market. That analysis may also include some forms of entry. Firms that would rapidly and easily enter the market in response to a SSNIP are market participants and may be assigned market shares. See Sections 5.1 and 5.2. Firms that have, prior to the merger, committed to entering the market also will normally be treated as market participants. See Section 5.1. This section concerns entry or adjustments to pre-existing entry plans that are induced by the merger.

As part of their full assessment of competitive effects, the Agencies consider entry into the relevant market. The prospect of entry into the relevant market will alleviate concerns about adverse competitive effects only if such entry will deter or counteract any competitive effects of concern so the merger will not substantially harm customers.

The Agencies consider the actual history of entry into the relevant market and give substantial weight to this evidence. Lack of successful and effective entry in the face of non-transitory increases in the margins earned on products in the relevant market tends to suggest that successful entry is slow or difficult. Market values of incumbent firms greatly exceeding the replacement costs of their tangible assets may indicate that these firms have valuable intangible assets, which may be difficult or time consuming for an entrant to replicate.

A merger is not likely to enhance market power if entry into the market is so easy that the merged firm and its remaining rivals in the market, either unilaterally or collectively, could not profitably raise price or otherwise reduce competition compared to the level that would prevail in the absence of the merger. Entry is that easy if entry would be timely, likely, and sufficient in its magnitude, character, and scope to deter or counteract the competitive effects of concern.

The Agencies examine the timeliness, likelihood, and sufficiency of the entry efforts an entrant might practically employ. An entry effort is defined by the actions the firm must undertake to produce and sell in the market. Various elements of the entry effort will be considered. These elements can include: planning, design, and management; permitting, licensing, or other approvals; construction, debugging, and operation of production facilities; and promotion (including necessary introductory discounts), marketing, distribution, and satisfaction of customer testing and qualification requirements. Recent examples of entry, whether successful or unsuccessful, generally provide the starting point for identifying the elements of practical entry efforts. They also can be informative regarding the scale necessary for an entrant to be successful, the presence or absence of entry barriers, the factors that influence the timing of entry, the costs and risk associated with entry, and the sales opportunities realistically available to entrants.

If the assets necessary for an effective and profitable entry effort are widely available, the Agencies will not necessarily attempt to identify which firms might enter. Where an identifiable set of firms appears to have necessary assets that others lack, or to have particularly strong incentives to enter, the Agencies focus their entry analysis on those firms. Firms operating in adjacent or complementary markets, or large customers themselves, may be best placed to enter. However, the Agencies will not presume that a powerful firm in an adjacent market or a large customer will enter the relevant market unless there is reliable evidence supporting that conclusion.

In assessing whether entry will be timely, likely, and sufficient, the Agencies recognize that precise and detailed information may be difficult or impossible to obtain. The Agencies consider reasonably available and reliable evidence bearing on whether entry will satisfy the conditions of timeliness, likelihood, and sufficiency.

9.1 Timeliness

In order to deter the competitive effects of concern, entry must be rapid enough to make unprofitable overall the actions causing those effects and thus leading to entry, even though those actions would be profitable until entry takes effect.

Even if the prospect of entry does not deter the competitive effects of concern, post-merger entry may counteract them. This requires that the impact of entrants in the relevant market be rapid enough that customers are not significantly harmed by the merger, despite any anticompetitive harm that occurs prior to the entry.

The Agencies will not presume that an entrant can have a significant impact on prices before that entrant is ready to provide the relevant product to customers unless there is reliable evidence that anticipated future entry would have such an effect on prices.

9.2 Likelihood

Entry is likely if it would be profitable, accounting for the assets, capabilities, and capital needed and the risks involved, including the need for the entrant to incur costs that would not be recovered if the entrant later exits. Profitability depends upon (a) the output level the entrant is likely to obtain, accounting for the obstacles facing new entrants; (b) the price the entrant would likely obtain in the post-merger market, accounting for the impact of that entry itself on prices; and (c) the cost per unit the entrant would likely incur, which may depend upon the scale at which the entrant would operate.

9.3 Sufficiency

Even where timely and likely, entry may not be sufficient to deter or counteract the competitive effects of concern. For example, in a differentiated product industry, entry may be insufficient because the products offered by entrants are not close enough substitutes to the products offered by the merged firm to render a price increase by the merged firm unprofitable. Entry may also be insufficient due to constraints that limit entrants' competitive effectiveness, such as limitations on the capabilities of the firms best placed to enter or reputational barriers to rapid expansion by new entrants. Entry by a single firm that will replicate at least the scale and strength of one of the merging firms is sufficient. Entry by one or more firms operating at a smaller scale may be sufficient if such firms are not at a significant competitive disadvantage.

10. Efficiencies

Competition usually spurs firms to achieve efficiencies internally. Nevertheless, a primary benefit of mergers to the economy is their potential to generate significant efficiencies and thus enhance the merged firm's ability and incentive to compete, which may result in lower prices, improved quality, enhanced service, or new products. For example, merger-generated efficiencies may enhance competition by permitting two ineffective competitors to form a more effective competitor, e.g., by combining complementary assets. In a unilateral effects context, incremental cost reductions may reduce or reverse any increases in the merged firm's incentive to elevate price. Efficiencies also may lead to new or improved products, even if they do not immediately and directly affect price. In a coordinated effects context, incremental cost reductions may make coordination less likely or effective by enhancing the incentive of a maverick to lower price or by creating a new maverick firm. Even when efficiencies generated through a merger enhance a firm's ability to compete, however, a merger may have other effects that may lessen competition and make the merger anticompetitive.

The Agencies credit only those efficiencies likely to be accomplished with the proposed merger and unlikely to be accomplished in the absence of either the proposed merger or another means having comparable anticompetitive effects. These are termed merger-specific efficiencies.[13] Only alternatives that are practical in the business situation faced by the merging firms are considered in making this determination. The Agencies do not insist upon a less restrictive alternative that is merely theoretical.

Efficiencies are difficult to verify and quantify, in part because much of the information relating to efficiencies is uniquely in the possession of the merging firms. Moreover, efficiencies projected reasonably and in good faith by the merging firms may not be realized. Therefore, it is incumbent upon the merging firms to substantiate efficiency claims so that the Agencies can verify by reasonable means the likelihood and magnitude of each asserted efficiency, how and when each would be achieved (and any costs of doing so), how each would enhance the merged firm's ability and incentive to compete, and why each would be merger-specific.

Efficiency claims will not be considered if they are vague, speculative, or otherwise cannot be verified by reasonable means. Projections of efficiencies may be viewed with skepticism, particularly when generated outside of the usual business planning process. By contrast, efficiency claims substantiated by analogous past experience are those most likely to be credited.

Cognizable efficiencies are merger-specific efficiencies that have been verified and do not arise from anticompetitive reductions in output or service. Cognizable efficiencies are assessed net of costs produced by the merger or incurred in achieving those efficiencies.

The Agencies will not challenge a merger if cognizable efficiencies are of a character and magnitude such that the merger is not likely to be anticompetitive in any relevant market.[14] To make the requisite determination, the Agencies consider whether cognizable efficiencies likely would be sufficient to reverse the merger's potential to harm customers in the relevant market, e.g., by preventing price

---

[13] The Agencies will not deem efficiencies to be merger-specific if they could be attained by practical alternatives that mitigate competitive concerns, such as divestiture or licensing. If a merger affects not whether but only when an efficiency would be achieved, only the timing advantage is a merger-specific efficiency.

[14] The Agencies normally assess competition in each relevant market affected by a merger independently and normally will challenge the merger if it is likely to be anticompetitive in any relevant market. In some cases, however, the Agencies in their prosecutorial discretion will consider efficiencies not strictly in the relevant market, but so inextricably linked with it that a partial divestiture or other remedy could not feasibly eliminate the anticompetitive effect in the relevant market without sacrificing the efficiencies in the other market(s). Inextricably linked efficiencies are most likely to make a difference when they are great and the likely anticompetitive effect in the relevant market(s) is small so the merger is likely to benefit customers overall.

increases in that market.[15] In conducting this analysis, the Agencies will not simply compare the magnitude of the cognizable efficiencies with the magnitude of the likely harm to competition absent the efficiencies. The greater the potential adverse competitive effect of a merger, the greater must be the cognizable efficiencies, and the more they must be passed through to customers, for the Agencies to conclude that the merger will not have an anticompetitive effect in the relevant market. When the potential adverse competitive effect of a merger is likely to be particularly substantial, extraordinarily great cognizable efficiencies would be necessary to prevent the merger from being anticompetitive. In adhering to this approach, the Agencies are mindful that the antitrust laws give competition, not internal operational efficiency, primacy in protecting customers.

In the Agencies' experience, efficiencies are most likely to make a difference in merger analysis when the likely adverse competitive effects, absent the efficiencies, are not great. Efficiencies almost never justify a merger to monopoly or near-monopoly. Just as adverse competitive effects can arise along multiple dimensions of conduct, such as pricing and new product development, so too can efficiencies operate along multiple dimensions. Similarly, purported efficiency claims based on lower prices can be undermined if they rest on reductions in product quality or variety that customers value.

The Agencies have found that certain types of efficiencies are more likely to be cognizable and substantial than others. For example, efficiencies resulting from shifting production among facilities formerly owned separately, which enable the merging firms to reduce the incremental cost of production, are more likely to be susceptible to verification and are less likely to result from anticompetitive reductions in output. Other efficiencies, such as those relating to research and development, are potentially substantial but are generally less susceptible to verification and may be the result of anticompetitive output reductions. Yet others, such as those relating to procurement, management, or capital cost, are less likely to be merger-specific or substantial, or may not be cognizable for other reasons.

When evaluating the effects of a merger on innovation, the Agencies consider the ability of the merged firm to conduct research or development more effectively. Such efficiencies may spur innovation but not affect short-term pricing. The Agencies also consider the ability of the merged firm to appropriate a greater fraction of the benefits resulting from its innovations. Licensing and intellectual property conditions may be important to this enquiry, as they affect the ability of a firm to appropriate the benefits of its innovation. Research and development cost savings may be substantial and yet not be cognizable efficiencies because they are difficult to verify or result from anticompetitive reductions in innovative activities.

---

[15] The Agencies normally give the most weight to the results of this analysis over the short term. The Agencies also may consider the effects of cognizable efficiencies with no short-term, direct effect on prices in the relevant market. Delayed benefits from efficiencies (due to delay in the achievement of, or the realization of customer benefits from, the efficiencies) will be given less weight because they are less proximate and more difficult to predict. Efficiencies relating to costs that are fixed in the short term are unlikely to benefit customers in the short term, but can benefit customers in the longer run, e.g., if they make new product introduction less expensive.

11. Failure and Exiting Assets

Notwithstanding the analysis above, a merger is not likely to enhance market power if imminent failure, as defined below, of one of the merging firms would cause the assets of that firm to exit the relevant market. This is an extreme instance of the more general circumstance in which the competitive significance of one of the merging firms is declining: the projected market share and significance of the exiting firm is zero. If the relevant assets would otherwise exit the market, customers are not worse off after the merger than they would have been had the merger been enjoined.

The Agencies do not normally credit claims that the assets of the failing firm would exit the relevant market unless all of the following circumstances are met: (1) the allegedly failing firm would be unable to meet its financial obligations in the near future; (2) it would not be able to reorganize successfully under Chapter 11 of the Bankruptcy Act; and (3) it has made unsuccessful good-faith efforts to elicit reasonable alternative offers that would keep its tangible and intangible assets in the relevant market and pose a less severe danger to competition than does the proposed merger.[16]

Similarly, a merger is unlikely to cause competitive harm if the risks to competition arise from the acquisition of a failing division. The Agencies do not normally credit claims that the assets of a division would exit the relevant market in the near future unless both of the following conditions are met: (1) applying cost allocation rules that reflect true economic costs, the division has a persistently negative cash flow on an operating basis, and such negative cash flow is not economically justified for the firm by benefits such as added sales in complementary markets or enhanced customer goodwill;[17] and (2) the owner of the failing division has made unsuccessful good-faith efforts to elicit reasonable alternative offers that would keep its tangible and intangible assets in the relevant market and pose a less severe danger to competition than does the proposed acquisition.

12. Mergers of Competing Buyers

Mergers of competing buyers can enhance market power on the buying side of the market, just as mergers of competing sellers can enhance market power on the selling side of the market. Buyer market power is sometimes called "monopsony power."

To evaluate whether a merger is likely to enhance market power on the buying side of the market, the Agencies employ essentially the framework described above for evaluating whether a merger is likely to enhance market power on the selling side of the market. In defining relevant markets, the Agencies

---

[16] Any offer to purchase the assets of the failing firm for a price above the liquidation value of those assets will be regarded as a reasonable alternative offer. Liquidation value is the highest value the assets could command for use outside the relevant market.

[17] Because the parent firm can allocate costs, revenues, and intra-company transactions among itself and its subsidiaries and divisions, the Agencies require evidence on these two points that is not solely based on management plans that could have been prepared for the purpose of demonstrating negative cash flow or the prospect of exit from the relevant market.

focus on the alternatives available to sellers in the face of a decrease in the price paid by a hypothetical monopsonist.

Market power on the buying side of the market is not a significant concern if suppliers have numerous attractive outlets for their goods or services. However, when that is not the case, the Agencies may conclude that the merger of competing buyers is likely to lessen competition in a manner harmful to sellers.

The Agencies distinguish between effects on sellers arising from a lessening of competition and effects arising in other ways. A merger that does not enhance market power on the buying side of the market can nevertheless lead to a reduction in prices paid by the merged firm, for example, by reducing transactions costs or allowing the merged firm to take advantage of volume-based discounts. Reduction in prices paid by the merging firms not arising from the enhancement of market power can be significant in the evaluation of efficiencies from a merger, as discussed in Section 10.

The Agencies do not view a short-run reduction in the quantity purchased as the only, or best, indicator of whether a merger enhances buyer market power. Nor do the Agencies evaluate the competitive effects of mergers between competing buyers strictly, or even primarily, on the basis of effects in the downstream markets in which the merging firms sell.

> *Example 24:* Merging Firms A and B are the only two buyers in the relevant geographic market for an agricultural product. Their merger will enhance buyer power and depress the price paid to farmers for this product, causing a transfer of wealth from farmers to the merged firm and inefficiently reducing supply. These effects can arise even if the merger will not lead to any increase in the price charged by the merged firm for its output.

13. Partial Acquisitions

In most horizontal mergers, two competitors come under common ownership and control, completely and permanently eliminating competition between them. This elimination of competition is a basic element of merger analysis. However, the statutory provisions referenced in Section 1 also apply to one firm's partial acquisition of a competitor. The Agencies therefore also review acquisitions of minority positions involving competing firms, even if such minority positions do not necessarily or completely eliminate competition between the parties to the transaction.

When the Agencies determine that a partial acquisition results in effective control of the target firm, or involves substantially all of the relevant assets of the target firm, they analyze the transaction much as they do a merger. Partial acquisitions that do not result in effective control may nevertheless present significant competitive concerns and may require a somewhat distinct analysis from that applied to full mergers or to acquisitions involving effective control. The details of the post-acquisition relationship between the parties, and how those details are likely to affect competition, can be important. While the Agencies will consider any way in which a partial acquisition may affect competition, they generally focus on three principal effects.

First, a partial acquisition can lessen competition by giving the acquiring firm the ability to influence the competitive conduct of the target firm. A voting interest in the target firm or specific governance rights, such as the right to appoint members to the board of directors, can permit such influence. Such influence can lessen competition because the acquiring firm can use its influence to induce the target firm to compete less aggressively or to coordinate its conduct with that of the acquiring firm.

Second, a partial acquisition can lessen competition by reducing the incentive of the acquiring firm to compete. Acquiring a minority position in a rival might significantly blunt the incentive of the acquiring firm to compete aggressively because it shares in the losses thereby inflicted on that rival. This reduction in the incentive of the acquiring firm to compete arises even if cannot influence the conduct of the target firm. As compared with the unilateral competitive effect of a full merger, this effect is likely attenuated by the fact that the ownership is only partial.

Third, a partial acquisition can lessen competition by giving the acquiring firm access to non-public, competitively sensitive information from the target firm. Even absent any ability to influence the conduct of the target firm, access to competitively sensitive information can lead to adverse unilateral or coordinated effects. For example, it can enhance the ability of the two firms to coordinate their behavior, and make other accommodating responses faster and more targeted. The risk of coordinated effects is greater if the transaction also facilitates the flow of competitively sensitive information from the acquiring firm to the target firm.

Partial acquisitions, like mergers, vary greatly in their potential for anticompetitive effects. Accordingly, the specific facts of each case must be examined to assess the likelihood of harm to competition. While partial acquisitions usually do not enable many of the types of efficiencies associated with mergers, the Agencies consider whether a partial acquisition is likely to create cognizable efficiencies.

www.ingramcontent.com/pod-product-compliance
Lightning Source LLC
Chambersburg PA
CBHW081312180526
45170CB00007B/2671